RELEASE THE POWER OF GOD'S

FORGIVENESS IN YOUR LIFE

By

Dr Felix Okeroghene Idolor

ISBN: 9798738024504

Published by: ZALINGRAPH SOUTH AFRICA'

Editorial Services by Heritage Editing Services

www.heritageediting.co.uk

THERE IS A FOUNTAIN FILLED WITH BLOOD
DRAWN FROM EMMANUEL'S VEIN, AND
SINNERS PLUNGED BENEATH THAT FLOOD
LOSE ALL THEIR GUILTY STAIN

– William Cowper, 1771

Contents

INTRODUCTION

*"'For My thoughts are not your thoughts,
nor are your ways My ways,' says the Lord.
'For as the heavens are higher than the earth,
so are My ways higher than your ways, and My
thoughts than your thoughts.'" Isaiah 55:8-9*

As human beings, we try to comprehend God with our limited understanding, but in doing that, we miss out on His nature and character. One area in which we have extremely limited understanding is that of God's forgiveness.

Forgiveness is limited from a human standpoint, but, with God, it is a powerful force. God's forgiveness does not just leave us where we are; instead, it comes with power to bring full restoration from sin and its consequences.

Jesus demonstrated this when healing the paralysed man in Mark 2:1-12. The Bible says "...when He saw their faith, He said to the paralytic man, 'Son, your sins are forgiven you.'" (v. 5)

With one statement, Jesus released God's healing power to that man. When the religious men of the day questioned His authority to forgive the man's sin, Jesus demonstrated that authority with the following words: "'But that you may know that the Son of Man has power on earth to forgive sins'—He said to the paralytic, 'I say to you, arise, take up your bed, and go to your house.'" Mark 2:10-11

Jesus demonstrated that God's forgiveness contains the power of full restoration by healing the man's paralytic condition. However, the enemy seeks to hinder us from receiving this gift from God.

In this book, we shall explore how to receive God's forgiveness and keep His power working in us. We will look at how to be restored from whatever damage the enemy has wreaked on our lives through sin.

As the Bible says in Lamentations 3:22:

Through the Lord's mercies we are not consumed,
Because His compassions fail not.
They are new every morning;
Great *is* Your faithfulness.

As you release the power of God's forgiveness in and through you, not only will His mercy, compassion and faithfulness become the daily song of your heart, you will enter into a new dimension of God's power.

CHAPTER ONE

Every Person's Need Of Forgiveness

The Comprehensiveness of The Gospel of Jesus Christ

"For I am not ashamed of the gospel of Christ, for it is the power of God to salvation for everyone who believes, for the Jew first and for the Greek." Romans 1:16

"For all have sinned and fall short of the glory of God." Romans 3:23

If there is one undisputed aspect of the Bible, it is that, as a race, we are flawed creatures. Humanity is generally in a fallen condition. We have all broken God's law in our relationship with Him and one another.

"For whoever shall keep the whole law, and yet stumble in one point, he is guilty of all." James 2:10

God gave the Ten Commandments to reveal to mankind that we are guilty and condemned law breakers who deserve punishment before the Divine Justice.

> "But we know that the law is good if one uses it lawfully, knowing this: that the law is not made for a righteous person, but for the lawless and insubordinate, for the ungodly and for sinners, for the unholy and profane, for murderers of fathers and murderers of mothers, for manslayers, for fornicators, for sodomites, for kidnappers, for liars, for perjurers, and if there is any other thing that is contrary to sound doctrine, according to the glorious gospel of the blessed God which was committed to my trust." 1 Timothy 1:8-11

From Apostle Paul's long list of offenders, you can see that everyone within the human family fits in one way or another. The commandments reveal our sinfulness and hold us all accountable to God for our actions.

> "Now we know that whatever the law says, it says to those who are under the law, that every mouth may be stopped, and all the world may become guilty before God. Therefore, by the deeds of the law, no flesh will be justified in His sight, for by the law is the knowledge of sin." Romans 3:19-20

The law reveals the knowledge of sin to all mankind so that, as we see our guilt before God, we can seek His grace and mercy.

Mankind's sinfulness began with the man and woman God created to sire the entire human race.

> "Therefore, just as through one man sin entered the world, and death through sin, and thus death spread to all men, because all sinned…" Romans 5:12

> "For as by one man's disobedience **many** were made sinners, so also by one Man's obedience many will be made righteous." Romans 5:19

The man these Scriptures refer to is Adam, through whose disobedience sin entered the world and by whom all were made sinners. The word 'many' refers to the entire human family. Mankind came under the mastery of sin through Adam's transgression.

The reason for this? In the beginning, God created Adam as the federal head of the human family. Adam represented all of us at the garden. He made every decision with us within himself, and then carried us into the consequences.

> "Then God said 'Let Us make man in Our image, according to our likeness; let them have dominion

over the fish of the sea, over the birds of the air, and over every creeping thing that creeps on the earth.' So, God created man in His own image; in the image of God created He him male and female created He them." Genesis 1.26-27

God created man in His own image and referred to the first person as man. The Hebrew translation is ADAM. That was not his name. Adam in Hebrew simply means mankind. God was speaking to all mankind as represented in Adam.

When he disobeyed God's command and ran away from His presence, God called to Adam in the following words:

"Then the Lord God called to Adam and said to him, 'where are you?'" Genesis 3:9

The Lord God was calling to mankind in Adam. The first man had carried mankind with him into his act of disobedience and the consequences were to come on them. From that moment, sin became the common, self-evident and undeniable reality of everyone in the earth realm, and with sin and offence come guilt, condemnation and alienation from God and our fellow man.

Now we know that whatever the law says, it says to those who are under the law, that every mouth may be stopped, and all the world may become guilty before God. Romans 3:19

Sin and its consequences are demonstrated in Adam and his wife Eve's first act of disobedience in the Garden of Eden; acts that remain prevalent in the human race till today. The only difference between that moment in Eden and now is that the consequences are more grossly amplified.

> "Then the eyes of both of them were opened, and they knew that they were naked; and they sewed fig leaves together and made themselves coverings." Genesis 3:7

For the first time, Adam and Eve saw their unfitness to stand in the presence of the same God whose fellowship they had enjoyed moments before their downfall. They became conscious of their sinfulness, and with that came guilt, shame, fear and subsequent attempts to hide from God. What a tragedy!

Sin fills us with a consciousness of guilt, condemnation and being unfit to be in God's presence. Nothing we do in our own intelligence and power can cure us of these. Sin-consciousness, guilt and condemnation make us behave like Adam and Eve when they sinned: we want to hide and avoid dealings with God. Yet, God keeps coming after us with His forgiveness and desire to restore us to fellowship with Himself. We see that when He visited Adam and Eve in their fallen condition, as well as from His conversations with them.

> "And they heard the sound of the Lord God walking in the garden in the cool of the day, and Adam and his wife hid themselves from the presence of the Lord God among the trees of the garden. Then the Lord God called to Adam and said to him, 'Where are you?'" Genesis 3:8-9

THE QUESTION OF THE AGES

"Where are you?" is the question of the ages; one for which humanity has been seeking an answer since the fall of our first parents in the Garden.

WHERE ARE YOU?

Let us examine God's first words to Adam and Eve after they fell. It is interesting that the all-knowing, ever-present God would ask where man was. Did God not know where Adam was? Certainly not. God asked the question to expose the consequences of sin to Adam, his wife and the rest of humanity after them.

By asking this question, God was asking Adam to look at what sin had done to him. This is always the first step to repentance and receiving God's forgiveness. We must recognise how far our sin and miserable condition have brought us. Only then can we understand the gravity and preciousness of God's forgiveness.

In the story of the prodigal son, the phrase, "…when he came to himself, he said… (Luke 15:17)" is used. His journey to repentance and restoration began when he came to himself.

Adam sins and God immediately sets him on the path to repentance by asking him the question that would reveal his fallen state. We only need a good look at the human condition today to see the depths to which sin has taken us; and how much we need God's forgiveness and redemption.

CHAPTER TWO

SIN AND ITS CONSEQUENCES

"Then the Lord God called to Adam and said to him, 'Where are you?'" Genesis 3:9

God came to Adam in the cool of the evening, calling out, "Adam, where are you?" This statement, as we are beginning to see, is packed with meaning. The Hebrew word for "where" also means "an island". Sin has made Adam an island. Adam and his wife, Eve, with the rest of humanity, became cut off from fellowship with God like an island in the middle of the sea. Sin breaks our fellowship with God and leaves us isolated and severed from His power, love, mercy and grace. It leaves us struggling with our weaknesses.

The Hebrew word translated "where" can also mean a place where one seeks shelter and refuge. Adam and Eve, perceiving that they were in danger and exposed, sought protection and shelter. Filled with a sense of fear, they sought refuge and shelter among trees with a covering of fig leaves. They were hiding from God.

The first words out of Adam's mouth were words of fear. "So, he said, 'I heard Your voice in the garden, and I was afraid because I was naked; and I hid myself.'" Genesis 3:10

This was the result of sin. It filled them with such a sense of dread and danger that they sought a hiding place. As William Shakespeare once said, "Sin makes cowards of men".

A great tragedy has taken place as a result of sin. Adam who, just a while before, stood boldly before God and confidently named all the animals brought to him; who heard God's voice and did not cringe, was now filled with dread and tried to hide from God.

This is what sin does. It fills us with fear and a sense that we are not safe. More importantly, it fills us with a dread of God. Adam and Eve, deceived by their own sin, now considered God to be the problem and, so, they ran from Him. We see this deception working itself out as they tried to hide.

> "So, the great dragon was cast out, that serpent of old, called the Devil and Satan, who deceives

the whole world; He was cast to the earth, and his angels were cast out with him." Revelation 12:9

"…but exhort one another daily, while it is called 'Today,' lest any of you be hardened through the deceitfulness of sin." Hebrews 3:13

Satan is the author of sin, which like its author, is deceitful. Submitting to sin is yielding to deception. Adam and his wife were now living in deceitfulness. When God called out to them, "where are you?", He was exposing sin's treachery to them. God's truth is the ultimate answer to all sin.

"Then Jesus said to those Jews who believed Him, 'If you abide in My word, you are My disciples indeed. And you shall know the truth, and the truth shall make you free.'" John 8:31-32

The truth of God's word liberates and empowers us to live free. Adam and Eve, seeing God through the lens of deception, ran because they thought He was their problem. In reality, despite their sin, God continued to love and seek their fellowship by visiting them. Never allow sin to chase you away from God. In moments of failure, seek refuge in Jesus. God is for you, not against you.

"What then shall we say to these things? If God is for us, who can be against us?" Romans 8:31

We see Adam and Eve in fear and danger, naked and powerless, seeking shelter and covering themselves with leaves from a fig tree. What a miserable condition to be in! Cut off from God and his power, the husband and wife tried meeting their needs by their own ability. Sin puts us in a position where we struggle, using our power and intelligence to do life apart from God.

> "Thus, says the Lord: 'Cursed is the man who trusts in man and makes flesh his strength, whose heart departs from the Lord. For he shall be like a shrub in the desert, and shall not see when good comes, but shall inhabit the parched places in the wilderness, in a salt land which is not inhabited.'"
> Jeremiah 17:5-6

Sin's awfulness, as described above, began with Adam's transgression in the Garden of Eden. It does this to all of us until we come to repentance through Jesus Christ. Adam ran away from God's presence, but we should run to Jesus for refuge.

Rock of Ages, cleft for me,

Let me hide myself in Thee;

Let the water and the blood,

From Thy riven side which flowed,

Be of sin the double cure,

Cleanse me from its guilt and power.

(Reverend Augustus Toplady 1763)

THE PAIN AND SORROW OF SIN

The Hebrew word translated "where" also means woe, sorrow and alas! It is an exclamation of weariness and grief; it is an imitative word, like saying 'ouch' when pierced with something that causes a sharp pain. Sin brings sorrow, grief, toil, weariness and pain into our lives.

God was saying, "Adam, you have condemned yourself to a life of pain, toil, sorrow, grief, and labour; to doing life in your own power and effort until you wear yourself out." When we live in sin we live in sorrow, grief, pain, weariness. Life is all toil and labour, sorrow and pain that includes all the sickness and disease anybody could possibly experience. God never planned for anybody to live this way.

"Then I returned and considered all the oppression that is done under the sun: And look! The tears of the oppressed, but they have no comforter— On the side of their oppressors *there is* power, but they have no comforter. Therefore, I praised the dead who were already dead, more than the living who are still alive. Yet, better than both *is he* who has never existed, who has not seen the evil work that is done under the sun." Ecclesiastes 4:1-3

Adam's sin brought all mankind under the tyranny of Satan's oppression that makes life unbearable. Acts 10:38 tells us that every sickness and disease results from his regime which sin brought about. The writer of Ecclesiastes laments that it would have been better not to even be born into a world filled with such oppressive conditions. Why? Because it is a complete deviation from God's design and plan for every human being.

Thank God that He did not leave us in this abject state but chose to send His Son to our rescue.

> "Inasmuch then as the children have partaken of flesh and blood, He Himself likewise shared in the same, that through death He might destroy him who had the power of death, that is, the devil, and release those who through fear of death were all their lifetime subject to bondage." Hebrews 2:14-15

Thank God that we can enjoy the life God designed for us to live by His power. John 10:10 in the Passion translation tells us that "A thief has only one thing in mind—he wants to steal, slaughter, and destroy. But I have come to *give you everything in abundance, more than you expect*—life in its fullness until you overflow!"

We do not have to continue to live in sin, toil, weariness, sorrow, grief, pain, sickness and disease. We can repent of sin and enjoy the fullness of life in Christ Jesus.

LOST IDENTITY

You are probably beginning to understand what God meant when he said, "where are you?" to Adam. He was setting out the conditions for Adam and the human family's repentance and recovery. The first condition for receiving forgiveness and restoration is recognising the miserable condition into which sin has brought us.

To further exposit the question: "Adam, where are you?", we find that the word "where" also means "NOT" in Hebrew. In other words, God was effectively saying "Adam, not you." This is a tremendous statement. God was telling Adam and, by extension, all humanity, "This is not YOU! This is not the Adam I created, who lived in my presence and ruled over my creation!"

Sin had changed Adam into that which God had not made him.

Think about that. We often wonder what is responsible for mankind's dysfunctional condition. When you consider the crimes and evil man is capable of, don't you wonder why? When we examine the cruelty people can unleash on their fellow human beings – Adolph Hitler's attempted extermination of the Jews during the Holocaust – don't we exclaim, "Oh, God! Why?"

The answer is in that simple statement at the cradle of Eden: "Adam, where are you?" The truth is, this was not God's original intent for Adam – sin changed him and humanity. Adam, by that act of disobedience, had submitted to a new ruler, Satan, and taken on the devil's nature. This truth is difficult to take in, but even Jesus referred to the most religious men of his day as children of the devil.

> "You are of *your* father the devil, and the desires of your father you want to do. He was a murderer from the beginning, and does not stand in the truth, because there is no truth in him. When he speaks a lie, he speaks from his own *resources,* for he is a liar and the father of it." John 8:44

Through Adam's sin, Satan became the spiritual head of the human family and was able to breathe all the evils we see today into men's spirits and minds.

> "For out of the heart proceed evil thoughts, murders, adulteries, fornications, thefts, false witness, blasphemies." Matthew 15:19

By taking over the lordship of humanity, Satan gained the ability to instil his nature into the hearts of men, bringing about evil thoughts that translate into the rampant wickedness in the human condition. God never designed for us to live in this way, and He has made it possible for this to be reversed in Christ Jesus.

When we come under the Lordship of Jesus Christ, the situation is reversed. We can be re-born and receive life – God's nature – into our spirits. No one has to live a moment longer under Satan's rule and continue to manifest his evil nature.

> "But as many as received Him, to them He gave the right to become children of God, to those who believe in His name: who were born, not of blood, nor of the will of the flesh, nor of the will of man, but of God." John 1:12-13

Thank God, He has provided a way out and we can come under Jesus's lordship of love and life.

Sin is a terrible thing. Not only does it make us into what God never intended, we act in ways that are out of line with who we really are. One moment Adam stood face to face with God without cringing. He stood before all the animals and named them. He walked and lived as a king over all creation because God had given him dominion.

Immediately after sinning, he runs and hides from God, manifesting a fearful and timid spirit.

Even as a child of God, if you sin and do not repent or receive God's cleansing and restoration, that sin will continue working to make you someone you are not. It will breed fear, a sense of unrighteousness and make you cower with shame and unworthiness in God's presence.

CHAPTER THREE
RECOVER YOURSELF

"All unrighteousness is sin, and there is sin not leading to death." 1 John 5:17

The word unrighteousness derives from two words: "un", which means "NOT" and righteousness which is right standing or rightness. Unrighteousness means we lose the sense of right standing or rightness with God, due to a sense of wrongness within.

You see, we know it when we sin because we sense that something is wrong. Just as Adam knew he was no longer fit to stand in God's presence, sin-consciousness fills our hearts and the only way out is to ask for God's forgiveness and receive restoration.

"If we confess our sins, He is faithful and just to forgive us our sins and to cleanse us from all unrighteousness." 1 John 1:9

Confessing and receiving forgiveness positions us to recover ourselves and our true identity in Christ Jesus.

> "And a servant of the Lord must not quarrel but be gentle to all, able to teach, patient, in humility correcting those who are in opposition, if God perhaps will grant them repentance, so that they may know the truth, and *that* they may come to their senses *and escape* the snare of the devil, having been taken captive by him to *do* his will." 2 Timothy 2:24-26

Note that it says, "you have to come to your senses" or as the old King James puts it: "recover yourself". God will not do it for you. In other words, you have to take what God is offering, receive his forgiveness and, through the knowledge of His word, recover yourself. You come into your identity through knowing the truth. When you get a hold of these powerful and life-changing truths, you can start rising out of the common life into God's purpose, plan and design for you.

> "For I know the thoughts that I think toward you, says the Lord, thoughts of peace and not of evil, to give you a future and a hope." Jeremiah 29:11

Evil was never God's plan for anyone. The Hebrew word for evil means that which is broken and no longer functions according to design. The present broken and dysfunctional condition of mankind was never God's intention and He wants to restore everyone to the original plan and design. However, He will not force it on us – we have to receive the forgiveness and restoration He offers in Christ Jesus.

LOST AS A RESULT OF SIN

The Hebrew word translated "where" can also be translated "which", "who" and "where". God was saying to Adam after he had disobeyed Him: "Adam, which are you?" "Where are you?" and "Who are you?"

This signifies the lost condition into which Adam plunged himself as a result of sin. He also plunged humanity into not knowing who we really are as a species compared to other classes of God's creation and in relation to God.

Adam's sin led to mankind losing their bearing when it comes to God and life in general. This sense of lostness pervades all mankind. Oh, how mankind has toiled through the ages to find answers apart from God! Every religion on earth is here because of man's search for the answers to "Who are we?" "Which are we?" and "Where are we?" Religion is man's quest to navigate his way out of this lost condition. All philosophical searches are an attempt to answer the questions God asked Adam in Eden. The universal pursuit of meaning in life seeks to answer the questions: "Who am I?" "Why am I here?" "How did I get here?" "Where am I?" and "How do I get from here to where I ought to be?"

We are the only created species preoccupied with this. Without sin, Adam enjoyed full fellowship with God and did not have such queries within him. He knew exactly who he was, why he was (his purpose) and where he was in relationship to God and the rest of creation. His act of deliberate disobedience to God's commandment cost him and the rest of mankind this differentiation.

Thank God for the good news of the gospel! By giving us Jesus in answer to these questions, God has not left us ignorant. God's forgiveness or pardon releases us from sin and delivers us from its consequences.

> "...for the Son of Man has come to seek and to save that which was lost." Luke 19:10

By receiving God's forgiveness, we can now walk in fellowship with God through Jesus Christ and enjoy a life with meaning., fulfilling His purpose for our lives.

GOD'S OFFER OF UNCONDITIONAL FORGIVENESS

> "This *is* a faithful saying and worthy of all acceptance, that Christ Jesus came into the world to

save sinners, of whom I am chief. However, for this reason I obtained mercy, that in me first Jesus Christ might show all longsuffering, as a pattern to those who are going to believe on Him for everlasting life." 1 Timothy 1:15-16

Jesus Christ brought God's offer of unconditional pardon to the world.

"For God so loved the world that He gave His only begotten Son, that whoever believes in Him should not perish but have everlasting life. **For God did not send His Son into the world to condemn the world,** but that the world through Him might be saved. He who believes in Him is not condemned; but he who does not believe is condemned already, because he has not believed in the name of the only begotten Son of God. And this is the condemnation, that the light has come into the world, and men loved darkness rather than light, because their deeds were evil." John 3:16-19

A more literal translation would be, "God did not send the Son to judge the world". When we are to be judged, we are arrayed before the courts of justice and held accountable for our sinful deeds. That brings about condemnation and we are made to pay for our sinful actions. If you notice, God always takes the initiative and reaches out to man with a plan to bail him out of sin and its aftermath. In the Garden of Eden, Adam, of his own free will and choice, broke the commandments knowing the full consequences. Yet, God, as we saw earlier, came looking for him and showed him the way back into fellowship.

Religion gives a picture of a stern and angry God who is unwilling to forgive. It portrays Him as someone who must be pacified and persuaded to forgive. However, the God we see in the Scriptures is always reaching out and offering humanity His unconditional pardon, beginning at Eden and culminating in the sending of Jesus Christ.

In the Garden, we see the beginnings of God's offer of unconditional pardon to mankind as He takes an animal, slaughters it and uses its skin as a covering of Adam and his wife. This prophetic act foreshadowed God sending Jesus as the sacrificial lamb for man's salvation; an offer that is available to all. The problem is not on God's side. It falls to man to accept God's offer.

Religion has always transmitted wrong ideas about God that have stood in the way of people appropriating and releasing the power of His forgiveness into their lives.

CHAPTER FOUR

RECEIVING GOD'S FORGIVENESS

The first and foremost way into God's forgiveness is to receive Jesus Christ as your Lord and Saviour. As we saw earlier in this book, Adam's disobedience in the Garden made all mankind sinners. Our subsequent acts of sin were simply fruits of an underlying sinful nature.

> "For as by one man's disobedience, many were made sinners, so also by one Man's obedience, many will be made righteous." Romans 5:19

We became sinners under Adam; sinfulness became our nature and our sins, mere fruitage of that nature. There is no use confessing sins in that condition. What everyone needs is a radical change of nature; to move out of Satan's lordship into the Lordship of Jesus Christ.

Jesus gives us the principle in Matthew 12:33: "Either make the tree good, and its fruit good, or else make the tree bad and its fruit bad; for a tree is known by *its* fruit."

If the tree is bad, its fruit will automatically be bad. It is no use trying to change the fruit – you must dig out the entire tree and replace it with a good one. This is what every sinful person requires and what God offers in Christ Jesus.

"Most assuredly, I say to you, he who hears My word and believes in Him who sent Me has everlasting life, and shall not come into judgment, but has passed from death into life." John 5:24

Jesus gives us the answer to the sin problem right here. LIFE. The English translation reads "everlasting life" which gives the impression that it refers to life forever. But this is not simply life forever because man, being a spirit, is an eternal being. The Greek word here, *Zoe,* means life in its highest form—the life-nature of God. In fact, Jesus tells us that the Father has this life (*Zoe*) in Himself.

> "For as the Father has life in Himself, so He has granted the Son to have life in Himself..." John 5:26

When we confess Jesus as Lord, we move out from under Satan's lordship into a new life where we possess God's nature. This solves the sinner problem in us. Under the Lordship of Jesus Christ, we are now spiritually re-born or born again. Satan no longer has the right to dominate us with sin.

> "Giving thanks to the Father who has qualified us to be partakers of the inheritance of the saints in the light. He has delivered us from the power of darkness and conveyed *us* into the kingdom of the Son of His love." Colossians 1:12-13

> "Therefore, if anyone *is* in Christ, *he is* a new creation; old things have passed away; behold, all things have become new. Now all things *are* of God, who has reconciled us to Himself through Jesus Christ, and has given us the ministry of reconciliation." 2 Corinthians 5:17-18

God's answer to the sinner-problem is a new creation. When you become a new creation through Jesus Christ, you receive a new life, and once you allow that life to dominate you, sin starts to lose its hold over you. Becoming a new creation positions you to appropriate God's forgiveness and release its power in your life.

Romans 10:9-10 tells us how to become a new creation in Christ Jesus.

> "… if you confess with your mouth the Lord Jesus and believe in your heart that God has raised Him from the dead, you will be saved. For with the heart one believes unto righteousness, and with the mouth, confession is made unto salvation."

Now that we are new creations in Christ Jesus and children of God, we have to deal with the memory of sins, our slip-ups and failings.

THE MEMORY OF SIN

One of the biggest hindrances to attaining God's purpose and living life in its fullness is the memory of our past sins. This is one of the main tools the enemy carries in his bag of tricks. He used it against the apostles Paul and Peter and against king David. He will certainly use it against you as you strive to be all God wants you to be.

> "… lest Satan should take advantage of us; for we are not ignorant of his devices." 2 Corinthians 2:11

Notice here, the keyword is ignorance. Ignorance gives Satan an edge, and if you are ignorant of his tricks and devices, he will have an advantage over you. Fishing into and attempting to bring your past into your present to defraud you of God's plan is one of his favourite tricks. Once you know this, you have the tools of God's word to block him and rise up to be all God wants for you.

In the next couple of pages, we will examine the principles in God's word that enable us to walk in victory.

CHAPTER FIVE

GOD'S COVENANT COMMITMENT TO YOU

"Bless the LORD, O my soul; and all that is within me, bless His holy name! Bless the LORD, O my soul, and forget not all His benefits."
Psalm 103:1-2

The psalmist, David, speaks here of God's benefits bestowed on him by the covenant. The provisions were for Abraham and his seed or descendants. Therefore, David, as a descendant, could boldly and confidently claim his covenant benefits. By extension, those benefits belong to us also because of Jesus Christ.

"And if you are Christ's, then you are Abraham's seed, and heirs according to the promise." Galatians 3:29

As David enumerates the benefits, the forgiveness of sins is the first on the list.

> "Who forgives all your iniquities, who heals all your diseases." Psalm 103:3

God's forgiveness is at the top of the covenant benefits for a simple reason. You cannot access the other benefits without first receiving forgiveness. This is where the battle is fought, won, or lost. Once the devil can rob you of the reality of God's forgiveness, he can rob you of healing and every other benefit outlined in Psalm 103.

Right after forgiveness, the psalmist says: "Who heals all your diseases". The devil will keep you sick if you cannot appropriate the benefit of forgiveness. David himself fought the battle to appropriate God's forgiveness in his life. This psalm shows how he did so. He speaks of God's forgiveness as a "benefit". This strong term can only be understood in terms of covenant commitment.

A covenant is a relationship of total commitment sealed in blood. God offered His total commitment to all men when he cut a blood covenant with Abraham and then, ultimately, with the blood of Jesus. By calling God's forgiveness a covenant benefit, David was speaking of it in the strongest terms. He was saying, "God has completely and irrevocably committed Himself to forgiving me". Seeing

God's forgiveness this way makes it difficult for the devil to rob you of its reality.

A PICTURE OF GOD'S TOTAL COMMITMENT TO YOU

The Hebrew word for benefit is best understood in picture form. Ever heard the statement "pictures are worth a thousand words?" Well, God is conveying His total commitment in picture form so that it will continually stay in David's mind and ours. That way, as the psalmist says, we will not forget our covenant benefits.

The Hebrew word for benefit is from the root word *gamal*, which is also translated as "camel". When you picture the camel carrying its owner through a vast desert, God's total covenant-commitment to you becomes more vivid. Camels are the lone rangers and long-rangers of the desert. They are remarkable for their incredible longsuffering in staying with their owners, in the harsh conditions of desert journeys, through to the very end.

In that sense, the psalmist, inspired by the Holy Spirit, portrays God's commitment to him using the word "camel". The camel, alone with its owner in the desert, is a picture of God's unconditional faithfulness to us in our covenant relationship with Him.

Hebrews 13:5-6 outlines this covenant of commitment on God's part. Let us look at the Amplified (Classic) version:

> "Let your character *or* moral disposition be free from love of money [including greed, avarice, lust, and craving for earthly possessions] and be satisfied with your present [circumstances and with what you have]; for He [God] Himself has said, I will not in any way fail you *nor* give you up *nor* leave you without support. [I will] not, [I will] not, [I will] not in any degree leave you helpless *nor* forsake *nor* let [you] down (relax My hold on you)! [Assuredly not!]" Hebrews 13:5

This is the picture David has in mind as he lays hold of God's forgiveness. He is unleashing the power of God's total commitment to him in the face of his failures. As you do the same, that power will manifest in your life to destroy the works of the devil.

CHAPTER SIX

GOD IS FAITHFUL TO FORGIVE YOU

As a believer, if you commit any sins (everyone does), you can receive God's forgiveness through Jesus Christ, knowing, just like David, that the offer is based on God's faithfulness to His covenant word. We can know we are forgiven because of God's faithfulness to His promise, not because we feel forgiven or feel better after prayer. How you feel after confessing that sin to God has nothing to do with the fact that you are forgiven. You are forgiven based on God's word and His word alone.

> "If we confess our sins, He is faithful and just to forgive us our sins and to cleanse us from all unrighteousness." 1 John 1:9

Faithful means loyal: God remains loyal to His covenant promise to forgive us when we sin. This is the word "lovingkindness" in Hebrew.

Faithful means a "firm adherence to a promise or observance of duty[1]": God adheres firmly to His promise to forgive us when we ask.

Faithful means an "unswerving adherence to a person or thing, or to the oath or promise by which a tie was contracted[2]". God's oath is behind his word of promise to forgive, and He adheres firmly to His promise to forgive us our sins.

> "My covenant I will not break, nor alter the word that has gone out of My lips." Psalm 89:34

For God to not forgive you when you ask violates His word and covenant, which is impossible with God. Your victory is in holding fast to your confession of God's forgiveness when the devil bombards your mind with thoughts of past failures.

> "Fight the good fight of faith, lay hold on eternal life, to which you were also called and have confessed the good confession in the presence of many witnesses." 1 Timothy 6:12

Every battle has an area of concentration of forces that holds the key to the entire war. Whoever wins in that area

---

1 (Webster's Ninth New Collegiate Dictionary, 1989)
2 (Webster's Ninth New Collegiate Dictionary, 1989)

will likely go on to win the war. In Psalm 103:3, David unveils where the enemy concentrates his forces – the reality of God's forgiveness. The enemy's focus here is to deny you the reality of God's forgiveness because, if he wins here, he locks you out of every other benefit, including the future God has planned.

Winning this battle is also a key to unlocking the goodness of God in your life.

CHAPTER SEVEN

FORGET NOT!

"Bless the Lord O my soul and forget not all His benefits." Psalm 103:2

Have you noticed that the psalmist is speaking to himself – his soul – here? He tells his soul not to forget all of God's benefits. A particularly important principle for victory is presented to us here. First, realise that every person is a threefold being.

"Now may the God of peace Himself sanctify you completely; and may your whole spirit, soul, and body be preserved blameless at the coming of our Lord Jesus Christ." 1 Thessalonians 5:23

This Scripture makes it clear that man is a threefold being. Your **spirit** is your essential self; the born-again part of you that has God's life in it. Your **soul** is your thoughts, your memory, emotions, imagination and will. This part is not saved instantly but must be gradually renewed through the knowledge of God's word.

The human **body** is the house where the spirit and soul reside. The apostle Paul calls it an earthly house in 2 Corinthians 5:1:

> "For we know that if our earthly house, this tent, is destroyed, we have a building from God, a house not made with hands eternal in the heavens."

The soul and the mind are one and the same. David, in essence, was speaking to his mind, saying, 'Bless the Lord, O my mind, and don't forget His benefits'.

> "Therefore, lay aside all filthiness and overflow of wickedness, and receive with meekness the implanted word, which is able to save your souls."
> James 1:21

This letter from James the Apostle is written to believers who were already born again and 'saved', yet he instructs them to receive the word of God which is able to save their souls. He is referring to their minds, where the battle of life rages. That is where the enemy attacks and is why the psalmist David, fighting the battle to actualise God's forgiveness, commands his **soul** not to "forget all his benefits!"

We all have to fight this battle to release the power of God's forgiveness in our lives. Everyone who has ever gone on to accomplish great things in the Kingdom has had to do this.

TAKE CONTROL OF YOUR MIND

The soul, or the mind, is the arena of the battle to walk in God's forgiveness and every other provision available to us in Christ. By talking to his soul in Psalm 103, David is taking control of his thought life. If he does not do that, other thoughts will displace the awareness of God's forgiveness from his mind.

> "…For though we walk in the flesh, we do not war according to the flesh. For the weapons of our warfare *are* not carnal but mighty in God for pulling down strongholds, casting down arguments and every high thing that exalts itself against the knowledge of God…" 2 Corinthians 10:3

Since the soul is the arena of warfare, 1 Peter 4:1 speaks of arming yourself with the same mind, or more literally, arming yourself with thoughts as for war. Even when you have appropriated God's forgiveness, the devil persists in reminding you of the past and making you feel you are unforgiven. The battle here is to take charge and bring your mind in line with God's word, by declaring with your own mouth that you are cleansed and forgiven.

David is doing this with his words. -By speaking to his mind, he is taking control of his thoughts. You cannot speak one thing and think another at the same time.

Try this brief exercise right now. Start thinking through the alphabet: A, B, C, D, E, F G, H, I, J, K, L and then right in the middle of this, start counting out loud: 1, 2, 3, 4, 5, 6, 7, 8. What happened with the alphabet? Your mind had to abandon that trend of thought and start counting 1, 2, 3, 4, 5, the moment you began to say the numbers out loud, etc. That is the power of the tongue which James speaks about.

> "Look also at ships: although they are so large and are driven by fierce winds, they are turned by a very small rudder wherever the pilot desires. Even so the tongue is a little member and boasts great things. See how great a forest a little fire kindles!" James 3:4-5

The tongue is the rudder by which you can set the direction for your thoughts, emotions and imagination. As the enemy tries to flood his mind with images of the past, David takes control with his tongue and thinks in line with God's faithfulness and forgiveness, thus re-wiring his memory from his past failures to God's present and eternal faithfulness.

> "My heart is overflowing with a good theme; I recite my composition concerning the King; my tongue is the pen of a ready writer." Psalm 45:1

That is what your tongue is: the pen of a ready writer. With it, you write the thoughts you want to think on the canvas of your mind. By confessing the words, "He forgives my iniquities" during the battle of his mind, David was saying "I choose to think of God's covenant commitment and His unqualified forgiveness towards me". He is replacing the memory of the past with the reality of God's present forgiveness.

"My tongue *is* the pen of a ready writer." The Hebrew word for **tongue** here can also mean an artist's paintbrush. Remember, the imagination is part of the soul, which is where the devil attacks in his attempt to keep you bound to the past. Now David uses his tongue as a paintbrush and begins to replace images of his past with new ones of himself forgiven by God.

CHAPTER EIGHT

FROM NEGATIVE TO POSITIVE SELF-TALK

David understood the principle and power of the tongue as the pen of a ready writer. If he continued to engage in negative self-talk, God's forgiveness would not mean anything to him, so he changed his self-talk to that of a forgiven man. It is the same for every one of us.

The reason many do not experience God's power of forgiveness is because they keep engaging in negative talk about themselves; and recalling their past with their words. The principle of positive self-talk is all over the Scriptures and it is powerful enough to transform your life.

> "This Book of the Law shall not depart from your mouth, but you shall meditate in it day and night, that you may observe to do according to all that is written in it. For then you will make your way

prosperous, and then you will have good success."
Joshua 1:8

This Scripture gives the key to success: the book of the law – God's word – shall not depart from our mouths. In other words, speak God's word continuously. Also, constantly meditate on the word. The Hebrew word for "meditate" means to mutter something to yourself. That is your self-talk. It is primarily saying it to your own hearing until a new image emerges that governs the way you act. This is why the passage goes on to say, "you shall observe to do according to what is written in it."

Guess what is written in it? "He forgives all my iniquities and heals all my diseases." You must begin to act according to that Scripture – as one truly forgiven of all his failings before God.

"...in whom we have redemption through His blood, the forgiveness of sins." Colossians 1:14

Notice it says we have forgiveness of our sins in Christ Jesus **now**. Let that be your meditation all day.

"Let the words of my mouth and the meditation of my heart be acceptable in Your sight, O Lord, my strength and my Redeemer." Psalm 19:14

Words that nullify God's word on earth are not acceptable to Him. God has declared you forgiven. You cannot turn around and call yourself unforgiven, wallow in self- pity and talk down on yourself. The "words of your mouth", your self-talk, must agree with God's declarations about you.

SPEAK GOD'S WORD TO YOURSELF

> "But if we walk in the light as He is in the light, we have fellowship with one another, and the blood of Jesus Christ His Son cleanses us from all sin." 1 John 1:7

Scriptures like this should be your self-talk and heart's meditation all day long. You can personalise it by saying, "I walk in the Light as He is in the Light. I have fellowship with the Father, Son, Holy Spirit, and my brethren, and the Blood of Jesus Christ cleanses me from all unrighteousness".

Notice that Psalm 19:14 refers to the meditations of your heart, not the meditations of your head. Just because a thought comes to your head does not mean you should speak it. Your head and heart are not the same. Your heart speaks of the inner man – your spirit – while your head is what you contact this world with. The enemy comes to flood your head with thoughts of your past. Provided you do not speak them out of your mouth, instead of going into your heart and becoming its meditation, they die unborn.

> "…and from Jesus Christ, the faithful witness, the firstborn from the dead, and the ruler over the kings of the earth. To Him who loved us and washed us from our sins in His own blood…" Revelation 1:5

Let this word of God be the words of your mouth and meditation of your heart. You can say "Jesus Christ loves me. He washed me from all sin in His own precious blood".

In Psalm 103, the psalmist, speaking to His soul, begins his positive self-talk with, "Bless the Lord, O my soul", and ends in verse 22 with the same statement. You should engage in this kind of positive self-talk to make God's forgiveness more real to you. Only then can its power be released in your daily life.

CHAPTER NINE

GOD'S MERCY AND FORGIVENESS

Under the inspiration of the Holy Spirit, David declares: "he **forgives** all your iniquity". To forgive, both in Hebrew and English, carries the idea of release. When God forgives us, we are released from the hold and dominion of sin.

The English word "forgive" meaning **to pardon**, was an original Latin word *"pardonare"* which meant to give thoroughly or wholeheartedly. In other words, "to grant freely". God's forgiveness has been freely granted to all in Christ Jesus. God has not placed any conditions on it. All we need to do is receive it.

To pardon is "to release from the legal penalties of an offense"; to absolve from the consequences of a fault or crime. When you receive God's freely offered forgiveness, you can also be delivered from the punishment due as a result of those sins. Today, many people believe they are suffering for their sins. That may be true, but, when you receive God's forgiveness you can also receive His deliverance from suffering.

> "Let us therefore come boldly to the throne of grace, that we may obtain mercy and find grace to help in time of need." Hebrews 4:16

This Scripture tells us that God's mercy awaits us, and the invitation stands for all to come and receive. Mercy is a force within God that makes Him not just forgive. He also releases us from the consequences of our wrongdoing.

Here is a definition of mercy which can speak to our hearts and help us draw on God's power to deliver us from the problems and difficulties we face because of our transgressions.

> "Mercy is the emotion aroused by affliction which comes undeservedly on someone else. It has special and immediate regard to the misery which is the consequence of sin and is the effort, which only the continued perverseness of man can hinder or defeat, assuage to entirely remove such misery." (Linguistic Key to the Greek New Testament)

This is a powerful insight. God's mercy is that powerful inward yearning within Him to not only forgive us but also to use his power to deliver us from the suffering, sorrow, grief and problems that come with sin and wrongdoing.

Notice, our definition of mercy says continued perverseness can defeat God's mercy. When you continue in sin and refuse to cooperate with God, the flow of His mercy and power can be stopped. If you cooperate with Him through His word, He will work within your situation to deliver you and resolve the issues sin has brought about in your life.

Yes, you may be in a mess as a result of sin, but God's powerful force called mercy is available to forgive and deliver you. We can see from Psalm 103:3-4 that God's forgiveness and His mercy work together:

> "Who forgives all your iniquities, Who heals all your diseases, Who redeems your life from destruction, Who crowns you with lovingkindness and tender mercies."

The JPS translation of verse 3 says "He redeems your life from the pit, surrounds you with steadfast love and mercy."

Sin is a pitfall that can make life hell on earth. When God forgives, He does not leave us to continue suffering in that pit. Instead, He reaches down to lift us out. But we must cooperate with him in making that deliverance real in our lives.

The Hebrew word "destruction" translated as "pit" in Psalm 103:3, captures everything the devil can do in our lives when we sin. The word means to lay waste, ruin, fall, harm, be abused, injure, be marred and to spoil.

Sin gives the devil space in our lives which he uses to carry out his destructive activities.

> "The thief does not come except to steal, to kill and to destroy…" John 10:10

God does not just forgive and allow us to remain with the rest of Satan's works. Mercy makes him intervene on our behalf to reverse whatever the enemy has accomplished. We see this mercy manifested in Jesus' life and ministry as He walked the earth.

> "Then Jesus went about all the cities and villages, teaching in their synagogues, preaching the gospel of the kingdom, and healing every sickness and every disease among the people. But when He saw the multitudes, He was moved with compassion for them, because they were weary and scattered, like sheep having no shepherd." Matthew 9:35-36

His compassion made him release God's forgiveness to the people; then he went further to reverse the works of the enemy in their lives by healing all manner of sickness and disease among them.

CHAPTER TEN

STRONGHOLDS OF THE PAST

L et us examine the words "forget not", which David used in Psalm 103:2, in some more detail.

When we look at the English word, 'forget', we see that it also captures the sense of the Hebrew word for forget. Forget comes from two words: "for" and "get". "For" is originally a prefix and building block in the English language denoting negation or exclusion. Here, it is attached to the word "get". Hence forget means "NOT- GET" or to lose your hold of something.

To forget God's forgiveness means you have lost your hold of it and all its accompanying benefits. Something else has taken hold and excluded God's forgiveness from your mind. It could be the memory of your past, sins, failings, guilt, condemnation or the sense of shame that continually fills your mind, pushing out God's forgiveness and the other benefits.

THE STRONGHOLD OF GUILT, CONDEMNATION AND SHAME

> "For though we walk in the flesh, we do not war according to the flesh. For the weapons of our warfare *are* not carnal but mighty in God for pulling down strongholds, casting down arguments and every high thing that exalts itself against the knowledge of God, bringing every thought into captivity to the obedience of Christ." 2 Corinthians 10:3

The old KJV uses the phrase, "casting down imaginations". According to this Scripture, the soul is the arena of spiritual warfare and the devil can build a stronghold in your mind.

Remember, the word "forget" in this context means something has "gotten a hold of your mind to the exclusion and negation" of God's forgiveness. That something is contrary to and cancels out God's forgiveness. If it has a hold of your mind, a stronghold is either being built or has already been built.

The devil can erect a stronghold of guilt, condemnation and shame in your mind, which is what the psalmist is dealing with here. He is fighting the enemy in his soul realm, either to keep him from building a stronghold of guilt, shame and condemnation in his mind, or to pull it down, if it is already established in his soul.

Spiritual warfare involves keeping the devil from erecting strongholds in your mind. If he has already built it, you can pull it down using word of God which is your mighty weapon of warfare.

The word "stronghold" in Greek, *oxuroma,* also means fortress and prison. Satan can make you his prisoner through the memory of your past failings, and the guilt and condemnation that comes with it. By allowing him to build this stronghold in your mind, you become his captive and cannot freely enjoy the benefits of your covenant with God. Once Satan locks you up in that prison, he can carry out his destructive works unhindered.

> "And the Lord restored Job's losses when he prayed for his friends. Indeed, the Lord gave Job twice as much as he had before." Job 42:10

The old King James version puts this as: "The Lord turned the captivity of Job…"

Look at Satan's destructive works in Job's life: he killed all his children, turned his wife against him and destroyed his businesses and everything he had; all because Job was held captive or imprisoned. He can do the same in your life if he can build that stronghold.

RECOVER YOURSELF

> "And a servant of the Lord must not quarrel but be gentle to all, able to teach, patient, in humility correcting those who are in opposition, if God perhaps will grant them repentance, so that they may know the truth, and *that* they may come to their senses *and escape* the snare of the devil, having been taken captive by him to *do* his will." 2 Timothy 2:24-26

If this stronghold, with all its negative consequences, exists in your mind, you need to recover yourself through repentance and acknowledging the truth.

> "If we confess our sins, He is faithful and just to forgive us our sins and to cleanse us from all unrighteousness." 1 John 1:9

When you repent and confess your sins, God is faithful to forgive and cleanse you. To allow the devil to keep your mind full of self-reproach and humiliation about your past is to say God is not faithful to keep His word, or that God lied and did not mean what He said or say what He meant. You are essentially saying God has broken His covenant, which is not possible. No! When God says He has forgiven you, count on it. You are forgiven!

Hold that in your mind all the time. Use that promise in God's word to pull down every memory of that ugly past the same way the psalmist did it. He used his mouth to repeat it over and over to himself.

> "I, even I, am He who blots out your transgressions for My own sake; and I will not remember your sins." Isaiah 43:25

God says He will not remember your sins. In other words, He forgets them once He has forgiven you. That should also be your attitude. Once you have received God's forgiveness for your sins, forget them and move on with God.

Allowing the devil to establish that stronghold keeps you stuck and unable to move into the future God intends for you.

> "For I know the thoughts that I think toward you, says the Lord, thoughts of peace and not of evil, to give you a future and a hope." Jeremiah 29:11

God has a whole great future planned for you but if you allow the devil to convince you that you are not forgiven, he will steal that future. So, begin today to recover yourself from the captivity and prison of a past that God has unconditionally forgiven. The blood of Jesus has cleansed you from all sin, guilt and condemnation.

"And they overcame him by the blood of the Lamb and by the word of their testimony, and they did not love their lives to the death." Revelation 12:11

The blood of the Lamb cleanses us from all unrighteousness, according to 1 John 1:7. Confess that continually, and victory will be yours in Jesus' name.

CHAPTER ELEVEN

EMANCIPATION PROCLAMATION FOR ALL

I n Luke 4:18-19, Jesus declares the following:

> "The Spirit of the Lord *is* upon me, because He has anointed me to preach the gospel to *the* poor; He has sent Me to heal the broken-hearted, to proclaim liberty to *the* captives and recovery of sight to *the* blind, *to* set at liberty those who are oppressed; to proclaim the acceptable year of the Lord."

Jesus came to proclaim liberty to the captives. William Beck's translation says, "He came to announce to prisoners: you are free."

Earlier, we defined the word "stronghold" as a prison. Satan can imprison you through your memories, but Jesus came to announce this: "Prisoners, you are free!" In other words, you can walk out of that prison a free person in

Christ Jesus. You can choose to walk out now, fully forgiven with God's unconditional pardon.

Jesus has announced your freedom from that prison. It is up to you to take your liberty and walk out of Satan's prison into the glorious future God has for you.

The Aramaic translation says Jesus was "anointed to preach to the captives, forgiveness". If the enemy has built a stronghold and imprisoned you with the memory of sin, Jesus came to announce forgiveness to you. That forgiveness is your release from prison. The doors are now open for you and it is for you now to take the step, get out and walk right into the glorious future God has mapped out for you.

On January 1, 1863, Abraham Lincoln made the emancipation proclamation, effectively freeing all slaves in the Americas. But do you know that the proclamation did not automatically translate into freedom for all slaves? A civil war raged within the nation to decide whether the slaves would or would not be free.

The same applies in your case and mine. The Lord has come forth and proclaimed all prisoners of sin free. It is up to us now to take the freedom that has been declared on our behalf. The slave master, the devil, will not give up any of his captives without a fight. When you decide to receive

God's forgiveness and claim your deliverance, the devil will attempt to fight you all the way. Your part is to fight the good fight of faith knowing that victory is assured.

> "For whatever is born of God overcomes the world. And this is the victory that has overcome the world—our faith." 1 John 5:4

Your faith is the victory in the fight to walk out of that prison into the glorious plan and destiny that God has for you. Hold fast to your confession that God has forgiven you; that God does not remember what He has forgiven, and that the Blood of Jesus Christ has cleansed you from all unrighteousness.

Faith's confessions create realities! As you hold fast to the confession of God's unconditional forgiveness, it will create that reality, in and around you, and free you completely from captivity to that ugly past.

CHAPTER TWELVE
FORGETTING THE PAST

The apostle Paul had to win the battle over the past to enter God's plan and fulfil his destiny. He describes himself as a persecutor of the church and the chief of sinners.

> "For you have heard of my former conduct in Judaism, how I persecuted the church of God beyond measure and tried to destroy it." Galatians 1:13

Paul, formerly called Saul, was so filled with hatred for the church, he set out to destroy it. The Greek word translated as 'destroy' here is a strong word indicating the wiping out of an entire city as in warfare. Paul was to the church what Heinrich Himmler was to the Jews in Europe during the 1930s. Heinrich Himmler was the main architect of the final plan that was supposed to wipe the Jews off the earth.

Acts 8:3 says "…as for Saul, he made havoc of the church, entering every house, and dragging off men and women, committing *them* to prison." The phrase 'made havoc of the church' denotes acts of brutal cruelty. In 1 Timothy 1:12-14, Paul had the following to say about himself:

> "And I thank Christ Jesus our Lord who has enabled me, because He counted me faithful, putting *me* into the ministry, although I was formerly a blasphemer, a persecutor, and an insolent man; but I obtained mercy because I did *it* ignorantly in unbelief. And the grace of our Lord was exceedingly abundant, with faith and love which are in Christ Jesus."

He describes himself as a former persecutor and an insolent blasphemer. These are some of the strongest terms to describe a person's character. He refers to himself as a blasphemer, the worst way a person of Jewish descent could characterise himself. Blasphemers in Jewish culture were condemned to hell with no hope of salvation. Then he called himself an insolent man. This word in the Greek translation speaks of someone who deliberately and contemptuously mistreats, wrongs and hurts another just to humiliate the person.

Such was the character of the man who would later become the great Apostle Paul of the New Covenant. No wonder he dubbed himself "the chief of sinners" (2 Timothy 1:15). To step into the office of an apostle and fulfil his destiny, Paul had to overcome the memory and sense of guilt, condemnation and shame his past brought to him. In 1 Corinthians 15:9 he tells us: "For I am the least of the apostles, who am not worthy to be called an apostle, because I persecuted the church of God."

No doubt, the devil did everything to remind Paul of that ugly past, build a stronghold in his mind and hold him captive. Paul had to learn to receive God's forgiveness and forget that past in order to fulfil his ministry and be a blessing to the church and the world. In 1 Corinthians 15:10, he gives us an insight into the power of God's forgiving grace:

> "But by the grace of God I am what I am, and His grace toward me was not in vain; but I labored more abundantly than they all, yet not I, but the grace of God *which was* with me."

He tells us that the grace of God was not in vain. If he had not released this power into his life, his feelings about his past would have nullified the grace of God and he would have remained bound and unable to fulfil his destiny.

Think about it! Paul wrote fourteen of the twenty-seven books in the New Testament. In addition to that, he took

Christianity beyond the shores of Israel into the Gentile world. If he remained shackled to his past, he would not have achieved so much by God's power and grace.

CHAPTER THIRTEEN

HOW TO FORGET THE PAST

Paul had to learn to forget and move beyond the past. That is the secret of his success and greatness. He tells us this much in Philippians 3:13:

> "Brethren, I do not count myself to have apprehended; but one thing *I do,* forgetting those things which are behind and reaching forward to those things which are ahead, I press toward the goal for the prize of the upward call of God in Christ Jesus."

He had to forget what was behind in order to reach for what lay ahead. If he did not do that, his past would have held him a prisoner, kept him from living out his full potential and robbed him of the great ministry God planned for him.

Now you may ask: "I see all that you are saying, but how do I forget the past with its ugliness?"

HOW NOT TO THINK ABOUT A RED MONKEY

If I told you not to think about a red monkey for the next 24 hours, what do you suppose would happen in your mind? Okay, spend the next couple of minutes not thinking about a red monkey. Yes! You got it right. You just spent all that time thinking about a red monkey while thinking about how not to think about a red monkey! That is how frustrating it can be. Telling you to forget about the past is the same thing. You cannot simply forget the past. Why? It is already part of your mindset.

That is the meaning of the word "remember". Think of the word remember as two words "re" and "member". In other words, it is to make it your member over and over again. The word remember means the thought comes to fill your mind over and over. That does not happen unless you permit it to run in your mind repeatedly. Like the apostle, you must do something to stop that cycle.

The English word 'forget', as we previously saw, means something gets a hold of your mind to the exclusion and negation of another.

That is exactly what the Apostle Paul did to be released from the past. To enter God's glorious plan, he had to fill his mind with God's assignment for him. His God-given dream became more dominant in his mind than whatever sins he had committed. The reality of God's unconditional love and grace was much more powerful, causing the past to lose its hold on him. He was free to move forward.

That is why He said in Philippians 3:13 (KJV): "... this one thing I do, FORGETTING those things which are behind, and reaching forth unto those things which are before..."

He forgot those things in his past and reached forward to the new dreams, visions and goals ahead of him. You cannot "not" think about a red monkey. The way to do so is to fill your mind with something else that would hold your attention much more than a red monkey would.

You, too, can forget your past this way by reaching out to God to fill your mind with a brand-new vision and dream for a great life ahead of you. Spend time consistently meditating on God's word until you can see yourself carrying out your God-given purpose in this world. We see this same principle unveiled in Hebrews 11:15-16:

> "And truly if they had called to mind that *country* from which they had come out, they would have had opportunity to return. But now they desire a better, that is, a heavenly *country.* Therefore, God is not ashamed to be called their God, for He has prepared a city for them."

As this Scripture says, "if they called to mind that from which they came, they would have had an opportunity to return." Going over past failures does only one thing: it sets a vicious cycle in motion by making you susceptible to opportunities to re-enact that past and further confirming you in a life of failure, guilt and condemnation. But notice what these heroes of faith did in order not to return to their past: they had to strive for something better. They became preoccupied with a heavenly dream and vision. The verse says they desired something better. In the literal translation what they did was much stronger than desiring. The Greek word used here means to stretch oneself out for something. It means to desire *and* strive.

God placed within them, just as He did for the apostle Paul, new dreams, visions, desires and aspirations into which they poured their whole lives and efforts.

To forget your past, you have to receive God's forgiveness and the cleansing of the Blood of Jesus. But more than that, allow God to fill your heart and mind with new dreams, visions, aspirations and desires. Then pour your whole life into reaching for their fulfilment in God's power.

CHAPTER FOURTEEN
RELEASED FROM REGRET

"Let your conduct be without covetousness; be content with such things as you have. For He Himself has said, 'I will never leave you nor forsake you.' So we may boldly say: 'The Lord is my helper; I will not fear. What can man do to me?'" Hebrews 13:5-6

One of the biggest roadblocks to living a full life, fulfilling our potential and becoming all God wants us to be is regret. Regret keeps us too unhappy and paralyzed to take steps toward the future. It strips us of the future and makes the horizons of our lives look dark and gloomy.

What is *regret* anyway? Let me define it to you the way it is in my heart, which has been immensely helpful to me. Regret is dissatisfaction in the present because of the mistakes and failings of the past. Regret is also a loss of confidence about the future for the same reasons. In other words, you feel there is no hope for anything positive in the future because of past failures. Regret breeds pessimism toward life.

It keeps us weeping over and over and unable to move beyond the past. The English word "regret" means just that. It means 'to weep over again'. In other words, your mind brings back the pictures and images of previous shortcomings and you weep over and over again as a result, which leaves you depressed, unhappy and stuck in that past.

In Second Corinthians, we see an example of regret which, if not dealt with properly, could have become a device the enemy can use to destroy the child of God.

We have here the story of a man who committed a sin of some kind. Some believe he launched an attack against Paul's ministry and insulted him personally, causing much sorrow to the apostle and the Corinthian church. The church proceeded to implement punitive and disciplinary measures on this individual and as a result he came to repentance. However, with this repentance came the temptation to be preoccupied and consumed with sorrow over his past.

The apostle Paul, inspired by the Holy Spirit, addressed this issue in 2 Corinthians 2:6-7:

> "This punishment which *was inflicted* by the majority *is* sufficient for such a man, so that, on the contrary, you *ought* rather to forgive and comfort *him*, lest perhaps such a one be swallowed up with too much sorrow."

Paul urges the church to help this individual overcome regret which was threatening to swallow him up with sorrow. Bemoaning past sins can cause you to be swallowed up with sorrow.

The word translated as swallow also means to engulf. Regret will engulf you with sorrow, stripping you of joy and leaving you without any strength for God's intended life for you.

> "Be sober, be vigilant; because your adversary the devil walks about like a roaring lion, seeking whom he may devour. Resist him, steadfast in the faith, knowing that the same sufferings are experienced by your brotherhood in the world." 1 Peter 5:8-9

Notice it says, "the adversary walks about as a roaring lion seeking whom he may devour". The word devour here also means "to swallow up" or "engulf". The enemy seeks those he can swallow or engulf with a spirit of regret. That way he can destroy God's plan for their lives and ultimately destroy them.

Verse 7 says to "resist him knowing that the same sufferings are experienced by your brotherhood in the world". The devil has no new weapons or ammunitions with which to fight God's people. He uses the same tricks and schemes he is trying on you with other believers all over the world.

You are not the only one being tempted to live in regret. He tries it with other believers. Those who rise to the level of God's purpose for their lives refuse to succumb to the temptation to wallow and be swallowed up with regret. They resist the devil stealing their future because of their mistakes.

Rise up now in the power of God's forgiveness and reach for the future God has for you. Refuse to be bound to the past. Do not allow yourself to be stripped of happiness in the present by being continually preoccupied with how you got to where you are. When you blame present circumstances on poor choices in the past, you are robbed of contentment in the present and hope for the future.

Hebrews 13:5 deals with this issue by reassuring us of God's eternal faithfulness. No matter how we got to where we are now, God is with us. He will never leave or forsake us. Therefore, it instructs us to "be content with such things as you have..."

Paul McReynold's literal translation puts it as "being enough in the present[3]". Being enough is having a sense of contentment about where you are now and how you got there. You are free from regretful feelings because you are assured of God's forgiveness and His faithful presence to take you further.

THE KEY TO HAPPINESS

This is the same principle Paul gives us in Philippians 4:11: "Not that I speak in regard to need, for I have learned in whatever state I am, to be content…"

It does not matter whether he got to where he is now through an error in judgment on his part. He has learned not to live his life preoccupied with his past and dwelling on his mistakes. That makes him content in his present circumstances. That is living with a happy spirit, whatever your situation. You can live with a happy attitude regardless of your circumstances, knowing that whatever your situation, however you got to where you are, God is faithful and will never leave or forsake you. He is *with* you to continue to work *in* you to perfect His plans *for* you. If you have this kind of attitude to life, you have power over your emotions.

---

3 (McReynolds, 1999)

Hebrews 13:5-6 in Kenneth Wuest's translation reads as follows:

> "Let your manner of life be without the love of money, being satisfied with your present circumstances. For He Himself has said, and the statement is on record, I will not, I will not cease to sustain and uphold you. I will not, I will not let you down. So that, being of courage, we are saying, The Lord is my helper. I will not fear. What shall man do to me?"

Let this Scripture fill your heart with courage to rise up and put the past behind you as you reach for God's great future for you. Do not let the devil use past failings to steal all you can be as a blessing to the world around you.

CHAPTER FIFTEEN

LOVE WILL NOT QUIT ON YOU

"So, David inquired of the Lord, saying, 'Shall I pursue this troop? Shall I overtake them?' And He answered him, 'Pursue, for you shall surely overtake them and without fail recover all.'" 1 Samuel 30:8

The story of David at Ziklag demonstrates how we can rise from the ashes of defeat to the highlands of victory and fulfilment if we learn to receive God's forgiveness and the power that comes with it.

Under tremendous pressure from Saul's persecution and desire to eliminate him, David succumbed to fear and decided to flee to the land of the Philistines. David knew fully well that God's plan was for him to be king of Israel, but, overwhelmed as he was, he failed to see how God

73

could perfect those plans. Instead of seeking God's guidance, he sought asylum with the chronic enemy of Israel.

> "And David said in his heart, 'Now I shall perish someday by the hand of Saul. *There is* nothing better for me than that I should speedily escape to the land of the Philistines; and Saul will despair of me, to seek me anymore in any part of Israel. So, I shall escape out of his hand." 1 Samuel 27:1

His escape with an army of six hundred men into the land of his own enemies was an act of failure to trust God. The Bible tells us in Romans 14:23 that whatever is not of faith is sin.

In the land of the Philistines, David suffered the consequences of not trusting God and taking things into his own hands. He had to fight battles just so that he, his army and their families could feed, and then he lied about it to the Philistine king. He literally lived a double life there as he struggled to make ends meet. Things came to a climax when David and his men were sent away from fighting alongside the Philistines on the battlefront for the simple reason that the Philistine army generals could not trust them.

David and his men returned to Ziklag, only to find out that the marauding hordes of Amalekites had kidnapped their wives and children, taken whatever else they could help themselves to, and then burned down the entire city. David was reaping the full consequences of his failure to trust God when he decided to flee to the Philistine kingdom.

1 Samuel 30:4, 6 tells us "…David and the people who *were* with him lifted up their voices and wept, until they had no more power to weep… Now David was greatly distressed, for the people spoke of stoning him, because the soul of all the people was grieved, every man for his sons and his daughters. But David strengthened himself in the Lord his God."

A spirit of sorrow and grief had taken over the entire camp and now they threatened to have him killed. They had reached the point where they regretted following David. This regret brought them to the brink of destroying the future that lay ahead of them when David became king. Never yield to a spirit of regret. It can take down, in a fit of anger, the future God has planned for you.

Confronted with mortal danger and extreme pressure, David handles this situation differently to the one that made him flee from Israel in the first place. He decides to face the situation with trust in his God.

Verse 6 tells us David encouraged himself in the Lord his God. While his army was being overwhelmed by grief,

David refused to be overwhelmed with the sorrow of regret. He had repented of his sin and knew his God had forgiven him and was still with him to take him forward.

Psalm 34:18 (TPT) says "The Lord is close to all whose hearts are crushed by pain, and he is always ready to restore the repentant one."

The situation looked hopeless, and the most natural thing to do was to throw his hands up in the air and give up on ever amounting to anything in God's plan. Instead, David does something amazing. Rather than surrender, quit and give up on his future, David takes the matter to God in prayer.

> "Then David said to Abiathar the priest, Ahimelech's son, 'Please bring the ephod here to me.' And Abiathar brought the ephod to David. So, David inquired of the Lord, saying, 'Shall I pursue this troop? Shall I overtake them?' And He answered him, 'Pursue, for you shall surely overtake *them* and without fail recover *all.*'" 1 Samuel 30:7-8

David realised only God had the final word on his future and his God-given dream. He would only quit if God called it quits on him. So, he took the matter to God. In so many words, he was asking: "Can I still pursue the dream you placed in my heart? Is there a future for me after I made such a mess?"

God answered in the affirmative. He commanded David to pursue, assuring him that he would recover all that the enemy had stolen.

We are in this world by God's planning and providence. His plan for our lives was formed before we were born.

> "Then the word of the Lord came to me, saying: 'Before I formed you in the womb, I knew you; before you were born, I sanctified you; I ordained you a prophet to the nations.'" Jeremiah 1:4-5

Before Jeremiah was conceived in his mother's womb, God already saw him and formed a plan and purpose for him. God is no respecter of persons (Acts 10:34). What He did for Jeremiah, He does for everybody else.

> "For we are His workmanship, created in Christ Jesus for good works, which God prepared beforehand that we should walk in them." Ephesians 2:10

Just like Jeremiah, God prepared a plan before the foundation of the world that He wants you to fulfil. Before you were born, God's purpose and plan for you was conceived. Knowing every sin and error you would commit, He still went ahead with His plan knowing His love and grace would see you through it.

David went to seek God because he recognised it was not his place to call it quits on God's plan for him. Only God has the right to decide when it is all over for us as far as His plan is concerned. As long as God has not pulled the plug, we have no right to quit on ourselves and the dream he plants in our hearts.

> "He who does not love does not know God, for God is love." 1 John 4:8

This Scripture tells us that God is love. The Greek word for love here is *agape*, the highest kind of love – divine love. William Barclay defines *agape* as "unconquerable benevolence and invincible goodwill"[4]. This love always seeks our highest good, whatever the circumstances. It is love that never gives up on us.

1 Corinthians 13:7 in The Passion Translation tells us this love "… is a safe place of shelter, for it never stops believing the best for others. Love never takes failure as defeat, for it never gives up".

Whatever your failures, God keeps believing in you and expecting His very best to come out of you. He never takes them as defeats and never gives up on you. It is up to you to take what remains of your life after all your stumbles, failures and sins, and surrender it fully to God. Accept his

---

4 (Barclay, 1964)

forgiveness and cleansing and go on to live the dreams and visions he has placed within you. God is faithful, and you can completely trust him to take your life and make something great out of it.

> "May God, who puts all things together, makes all things whole, who made a lasting mark through the sacrifice of Jesus, the sacrifice of blood that sealed the eternal covenant, who led Jesus, our Great Shepherd, up and alive from the dead, now put you together, provide you with everything you need to please him, make us into what gives him most pleasure, by means of the sacrifice of Jesus, the Messiah. All glory to Jesus forever and always! Oh, yes, yes, yes." Hebrews 13:20 (The Message)

CHAPTER SIXTEEN

FORGIVE AND WALK IN VICTORY

In Matthew 6:9-13, the Lord Jesus gave His earthly disciples the following prayer outline.

"In this manner, therefore, pray:

Our Father in heaven, hallowed be Your name.

Your kingdom come

Your will be done on earth as *it is* in heaven.

Give us this day our daily bread.

And forgive us our debts, as we forgive our debtors.

And do not lead us into temptation,

But deliver us from the evil one.

For Yours is the kingdom and the power and the glory forever. Amen.

"For if you forgive men their trespasses, your heavenly Father will also forgive you. But if you do not forgive men their trespasses, neither will your Father forgive your trespasses."

It is important, first and foremost, to know that the Lord Jesus is speaking here to Jews living under the Old Covenant. The New Covenant had not yet come into force because His blood had not yet been shed at the Cross. Hebrews 13:20 speaks of the Blood of Jesus as the blood of an everlasting covenant. We can see that Matthew 6:9-13 refers to a Jew praying under the Old Covenant; however, the outlined principles still apply to New Covenant believers.

What is Jesus speaking about in teaching the disciples to pray, "forgive us our trespasses as we forgive those who trespass against us" (v. 12)? The answer comes in verses 14-15 as the Lord continues teaching.

Verse 15 says "…but if you do not forgive men their trespasses, neither will your heavenly father forgive you your trespasses." Here, Jesus is showing how the sin of unforgiveness can hinder your prayers and affect your life.

Throughout Jesus' teachings about sin, the one He spoke about the most was unforgiveness. Why? It is the deadliest of sins. Every time Jesus spoke of faith and prayer, He touched on the subject of unforgiveness. In Mark 11:22-26, He clearly unveiled the power of faith. It can move mountains of any kind, and bring answers from heaven, where God is, to the earth, where men need them. Jesus would not finish this great discourse on faith and prayer without warning us about the sin of unforgiveness.

> "And whenever you stand praying, if you have anything against anyone, forgive him, that your Father in heaven may also forgive you your trespasses. But if you do not forgive, neither will your Father in heaven forgive your trespasses." (Mark 11:25-26)

Jesus separates unforgiveness into its own category by saying the heavenly Father will not forgive your trespasses if you do not forgive men. Unforgiveness is the one sin you cannot be forgiven from until you forgive.

Why did the Lord Jesus Christ especially mention unforgiveness with respect to your faith, prayer and entire life? Because this is where you will experience the greatest difficulty with Satan as you dare to live according to God's plans for you. Satan will get people to do things to persecute you, to say and do things that will hurt you.

WHEN YOU STAND PRAYING FORGIVE

> "And whenever you **stand** praying, if you have anything against anyone, forgive him, that your Father in heaven may forgive you your trespasses."
> Mark 11:25

Jesus used the word "stand" in relationship to prayer, followed by the requirement to forgive. The word 'stand' does not necessarily refer to physical posture in prayer. You can pray to God in any posture. Standing here refers to warfare in prayer. We can see that in Ephesians 3:10-13:

> "Finally, my brethren, be strong in the Lord and in the power of His might. Put on the whole armor of God, that you may be able to stand against the wiles of the devil. For we do not wrestle against flesh and blood, but against principalities, against powers, against the rulers of the darkness of this age, against spiritual *hosts* of wickedness in the heavenly *places.* Therefore, take up the whole armor of God, that you may be able to withstand in the evil day, and having done all, to stand."

In these verses, the apostle Paul, discussing spiritual warfare in connection with prayer, shows that our real opponent is not human beings, but Satan and his forces of darkness. Between verses 10 and 18, he uses the word 'stand' three times. If you add the word 'withstand' from verse 13, it comes up to four. That tells us that standing refers to warfare in prayer.

What did Jesus emphasise the most in this warfare against Satan and his forces of darkness? Forgiving others. When you are praying and believing for anything from God, this is where you could have the most difficulty.

The temptation to harbour unforgiveness in your heart is charged by demonic forces. You must resist it with God's power. If Satan can get to you here, your faith and prayer life will be completely shut down and he will gain the advantage. Jesus made it clear that the only way out is to forgive.

In natural warfare, the enemy concentrates his forces where the opponent is most vulnerable. If he wins there, he can take every other battle ground. Satan also concentrates on attacking you in this area because winning there gives him the entire battle ground. Unforgiveness will cost you spiritually, mentally, physically and materially. It allows the devil to place sickness in your mind and body from which you cannot be healed until you forgive. Satan can steal from your finances and work havoc in other areas of life through unforgiveness. In fact, if your prayers seem to be unanswered, check your heart to see if you are holding anything against anybody.

DEALING WITH OFFENCES

> "Yes, and all who desire to live godly in Christ Jesus will suffer persecution." 2 Timothy 3:12

If you desire the life God planned for you in this world, the Bible says you will suffer persecution, regardless of where you are pursuing this life in Christ Jesus. The enemy will attempt to persecute you.

Jesus put it this way in His teaching in Luke 17:1 '... "It is impossible that no offenses should come, but woe *to him* through whom they do come!"'

As long as you are alive, the enemy will ensure that you always run into opportunities to get offended at people. The important thing is to pass these opportunities by, while maintaining a forgiving heart. *Scandalon,* the Greek word for offense means a trap. Unforgiveness is a trap the enemy sets, and we must learn to avoid it by always having a forgiving heart.

The Hebrew word for persecute means "to pursue with a hostile intent", and John 10:10 gives us more insight: "The thief does not come except to steal, and to kill, and to destroy..." In other words, the enemy will attempt to come after you with the intention "...to steal, kill and destroy."

However, we do not have to be afraid and quit, "for whatever is born of God overcomes the world. And this is the victory that has overcome the world—our faith." 1 John 5:4

We are world-overcomers, and we can walk in victory over whatever the enemy comes against us with. The Bible makes it clear that the enemy has a bag full of tricks and he gets the advantage over us only when we fall for his tricks.

2 Corinthians 2:11 "...lest Satan should take advantage of us; for we are not ignorant of his devices."

One of his most potent tricks is luring people into unforgiveness. If he succeeds, he gains the advantage which he can use to steal, kill and destroy. We cannot afford to give him such an advantage.

As you read this, if anyone comes up in your heart against whom you hold any unforgiveness, stop for moment right now. Go before God, mention that person by name and confess your forgiveness for them. Then, listen for whatever action the Holy Spirit will place on your heart to take toward that person. The Lord might want you to call them up and ask for forgiveness if you are in the wrong. Listen to your heart and carry out God's instruction. Unforgiveness is a deadly sin that can get you into trouble and keep you there. Do everything you can to stay in the forgiveness and the love of God.

OVERFLOW WITH FORGIVENESS FROM YOUR HEART

Peter brought up this question of unforgiveness to Jesus in Matthew 18:21: "Lord, how often shall my brother sin against me, and I forgive him? Up to seven times?"

Knowing Peter, he was probably having difficulties at home with one of his brothers. As the Bible says, offences will come. The enemy will do whatever he can, including using your relatives, to get you into unforgiveness. Peter seemed to be repeatedly running into this problem, and finally asked Jesus how many times he needed to forgive his brother. Rabbinical teaching in those days limited forgiveness to three times, so Peter thought he was generous in forgiving his brother seven times. This is why Jesus surprised him when he answered: "I do not say to you seven times but until seventy times seven." Matthew 18:22

Seventy times seven is 7x10x7. That is an interesting concept because, in Hebrew, if you multiply any number by 10, you have the fullness of whatever that number represents. The number 7 represents completeness or perfection. Multiply that by 10 and you have completeness in full manifestation. Therefore, 7x10 in relation to forgiveness would mean the full manifestation of complete forgiveness. Then multiply that seventy by seven. That means taking something full and complete and making it full and complete all over again. What do you have, then? An overflow. Jesus was teaching Peter that he should overflow with forgiveness all the time.

This is how Jesus literally lived. He overflowed with God's forgiveness toward all people. He still overflows with that forgiveness today. He is the same yesterday, today and forever (Hebrews 13:8).

By expecting His disciples to forgive 70x7 times a day, Jesus was calling on them to overflow with forgiveness to all men. We are to manifest His heart of forgiveness to all men. This is the way to victory in all circumstances.

The Bible tells us that God's love has been shed abroad in Believers' hearts by the Holy Spirit.

"Now hope does not disappoint, because the love of God has been poured out in our hearts by the Holy Spirit who was given to us." Romans 5:5

Kenneth Wuest translates Romans 5:5 as "…and this hope does not disappoint, because the love of God has been poured out in our hearts and still floods them through the agency of the Holy Spirit who has been given to us."

From a natural perspective, it is not possible to forgive the way Jesus taught us to. It can only be done supernaturally, through the power of the Holy Spirit who dwells in believers. A flood of love and forgiveness residing in you is waiting to be turned loose in every situation and toward all people, enabling you to always walk in victory.

The Christian walk was always designed by God to be supernatural, not to be lived in our own strength. It is to be lived by the Holy Spirit's power in us. He enables us to forgive and be a blessing to people, no matter how they hurt us.

> "You are of God, little children, and have overcome them, because He who is in you is greater than he who is in the world." 1 John 4:4

You must become God-inside minded to walk in victory over unforgiveness. The person that offended and hurt you may be inexcusable from your perspective, and you might think you cannot and should not forgive. This kind of thinking will trap you in unforgiveness, allowing the enemy to conduct his destructive activities in your life. Look beyond your reasoning faculties to the power inside you to forgive supernaturally and walk in victory. The Holy Spirit is in your heart if you are a child of God.

Do not lock the flood of love inside you away from the world. Allow it to flow by releasing forgiveness to all who need it in your life.

Come before the Lord in prayer and say, "Heavenly father, [their name] has hurt me so badly that I cannot forgive in my natural power, but I can, through the Holy Spirit. I declare them forgiven from the bottom of my heart, and from this moment, confess that your love will flow from within me as a mighty river toward all men in Jesus' name."

Remember that the enemy will always bring back flashes of whatever that person did or said against you. Do not yield to such memories. Hold fast to your confession that the person is forgiven and act like you have genuinely forgiven them. You will soon see the power of God manifest more and more in your life and circumstances.

RECEIVE JESUS CHRIST AS YOUR LORD AND SAVIOR

Jesus is the embodiment of God's forgiveness to all mankind. You cannot really know God's forgiveness in your life apart from Jesus Christ. Only in submitting to and confessing Jesus as Lord can you walk in the reality and power of God's forgiveness.

The good news is that He has promised not to turn away anyone who comes to Him.

> "All that the Father gives Me will come to Me, and the one who comes to Me I will by no means cast out." John 6:37

Approach Him in humble submission. He will receive you and give you a new life, cleansing you in his precious blood from all your sins. Then you can begin life with God as though you never sinned.

> "But as many as received Him, to them He gave the right to become children of God, to those who

91

believe in His name: who were born, not of blood, nor of the will of the flesh, nor of the will of man, but of God."

If you will receive Jesus as your Lord and saviour now, the Bible says you will be born of God in your heart. He will impart a new life into your spirit.

"Repent therefore and be converted, that your sins may be blotted out, so that times of refreshing may come from the presence of the Lord." Acts 3:19

Then Romans 10:9 says, "… if you confess with your mouth the Lord Jesus and believe in your heart that God has raised Him from the dead, you will be saved."

Now, pray the following prayer sincerely to receive total forgiveness, cleansing, and the new life available to you in Christ Jesus.

"Heavenly Father, I come to you just as I am in the name of your Son, Jesus Christ. The Bible says as many as come to you through His name, You will not cast out. You will receive them and give them a new eternal life in Christ.

I repent of a life of sin. I believe with all my heart that Jesus took my sins upon Himself, died in my place on the cross and received the punishment due to me. I believe You raised Him up for my justification on the third day.

Today, I confess and receive Jesus as my Lord and Saviour. I believe a new life is imparted to my spirit at this moment, I am born again by your Holy Spirit and the blood of Jesus cleanses me from all sin.

I now walk in the reality and power of your forgiveness in every area of my life in the mighty Name of Jesus. Amen."

If you just said the above prayer from your heart in faith, Jesus Christ is now your Lord and Saviour, and you are a born-again child of the Living God. This is the beginning of a new and exciting relationship between you, Jesus Christ and God the Father.

WELCOME TO THE FAMILY OF GOD!

Please contact me at abc@abettercovenant.org or visit the ministry website at www.abettercovenant.org for more teachings to help you grow and take full advantage of God's provision for you as His child.

Wherever you are, please join a local church where God's word, the bible is taught and preached, and where you will have the support of a local network of fellow believers.

Bibliography

Barclay, W. (1964). New Testament Words . In W. Barclay, *New Testament Words*. Louisville Kentucky: Westminster John Knox Press.

Beck, W. F. (1976). The Holy Bible, An American Translation. In W. F. Beck, *The Holy Bible, An American Translation*. New Haven, MO: Leader Publishing Company .

III, C. R. (1998). Linguistic and Exegetical Key to the Greek New Testament. In C. R. III, *Linguistic and Exegetical Key to the Greek New Testament*. Grand Rapids, Michigan: Zondervan publishing House.

Jewish Publication Society. (2004). *The Jewish Study Bible*. (A. B. Brettler, editors, & c. e. Michael Fishbane, Eds.) Oxford , New York: . Oxford ; New York :Oxford University Press,.

McReynolds, P. R. (1999). Word Study Greek-English New Testament: With Complete Concordance. In

P. R. McReynolds, *Word Study Greek-English New Testament: With Complete Concordance.*

Webster's Ninth New Collegiate Dictionary. (1989). Springfield, Mass., U.S.A.: : Merriam-Webster.